W9-CBR-722

For the Love of *Pumpkins*

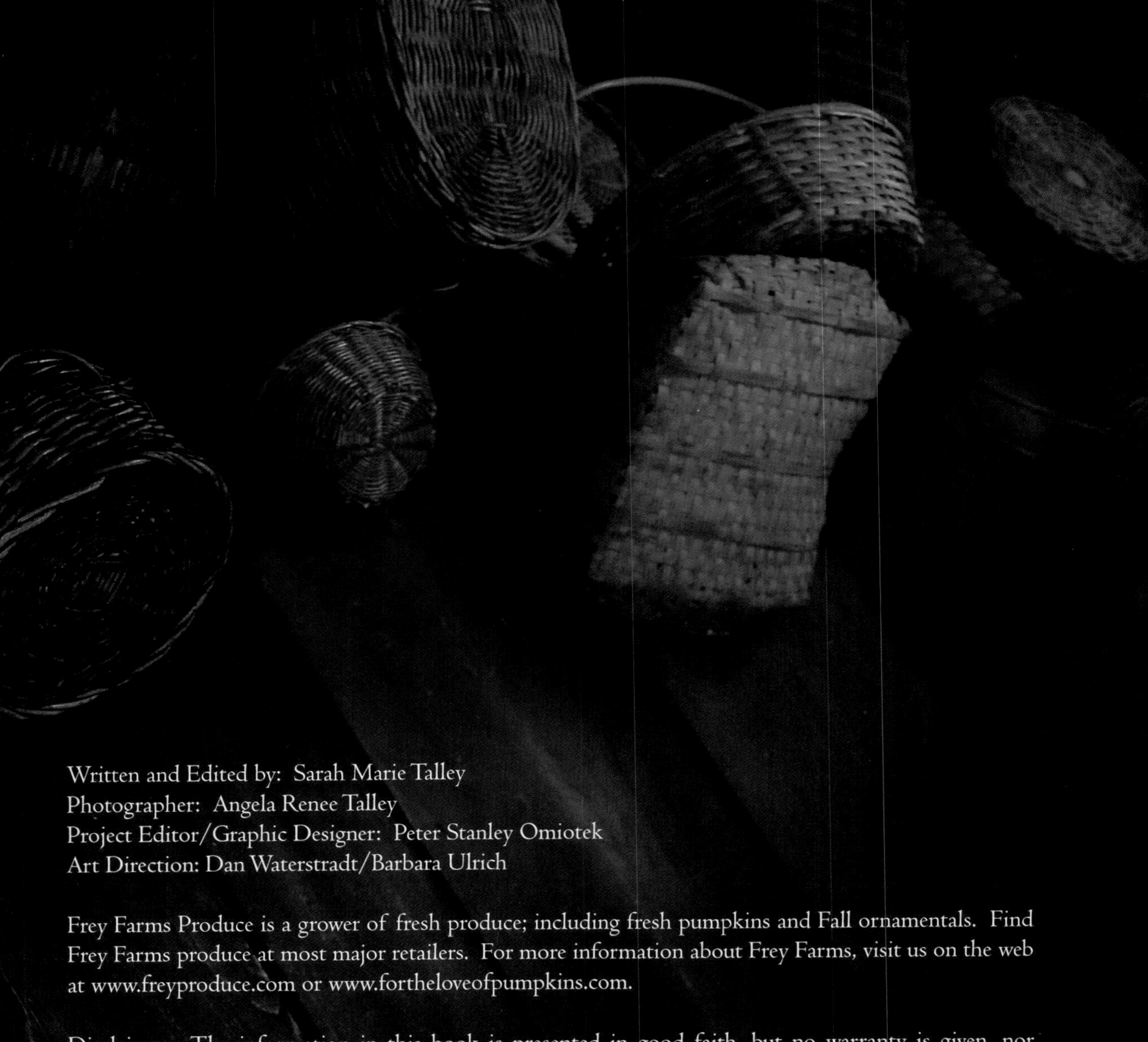

Written and Edited by: Sarah Marie Talley
Photographer: Angela Renee Talley
Project Editor/Graphic Designer: Peter Stanley Omiotek
Art Direction: Dan Waterstradt/Barbara Ulrich

Frey Farms Produce is a grower of fresh produce; including fresh pumpkins and Fall ornamentals. Find Frey Farms produce at most major retailers. For more information about Frey Farms, visit us on the web at www.freyproduce.com or www.fortheloveofpumpkins.com.

Disclaimer: The information in this book is presented in good faith, but no warranty is given, nor results guaranteed, nor is freedom from any patent to be inferred. Since we have no control over physical conditions surrounding the application of the information herein contained Frey Farms, the author, and related companies disclaim any liability for untoward results.

IMPORTANT: All activities involve a degree of risk. Skills, materials, and tools vary widely. Although the editors have made every effort to ensure accuracy, the reader remains responsible for the selection and use of tools, materials and methods.

Published by Frey Produce, LLC.
Rural Route 1 Box 89
Keenes, IL 62851
618-835-2536

ISBN # 978-0-9795342-0-1

Printed in the U.S.A

For the Love of

A Visual Guide to Fall Decorating with
Pumpkins and Ornamentals

Sarah Marie Talley

Photographs by Angela R. Talley

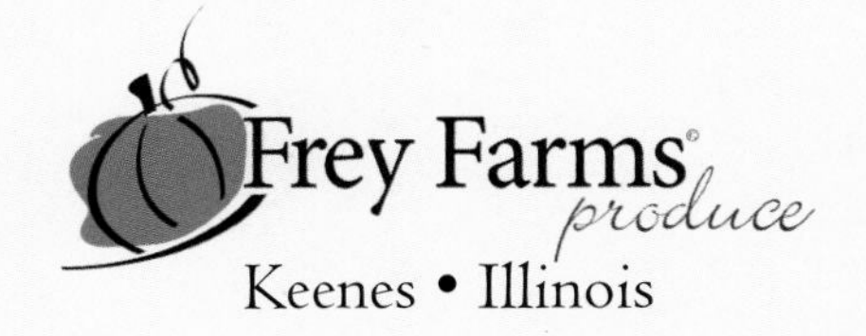

Contents

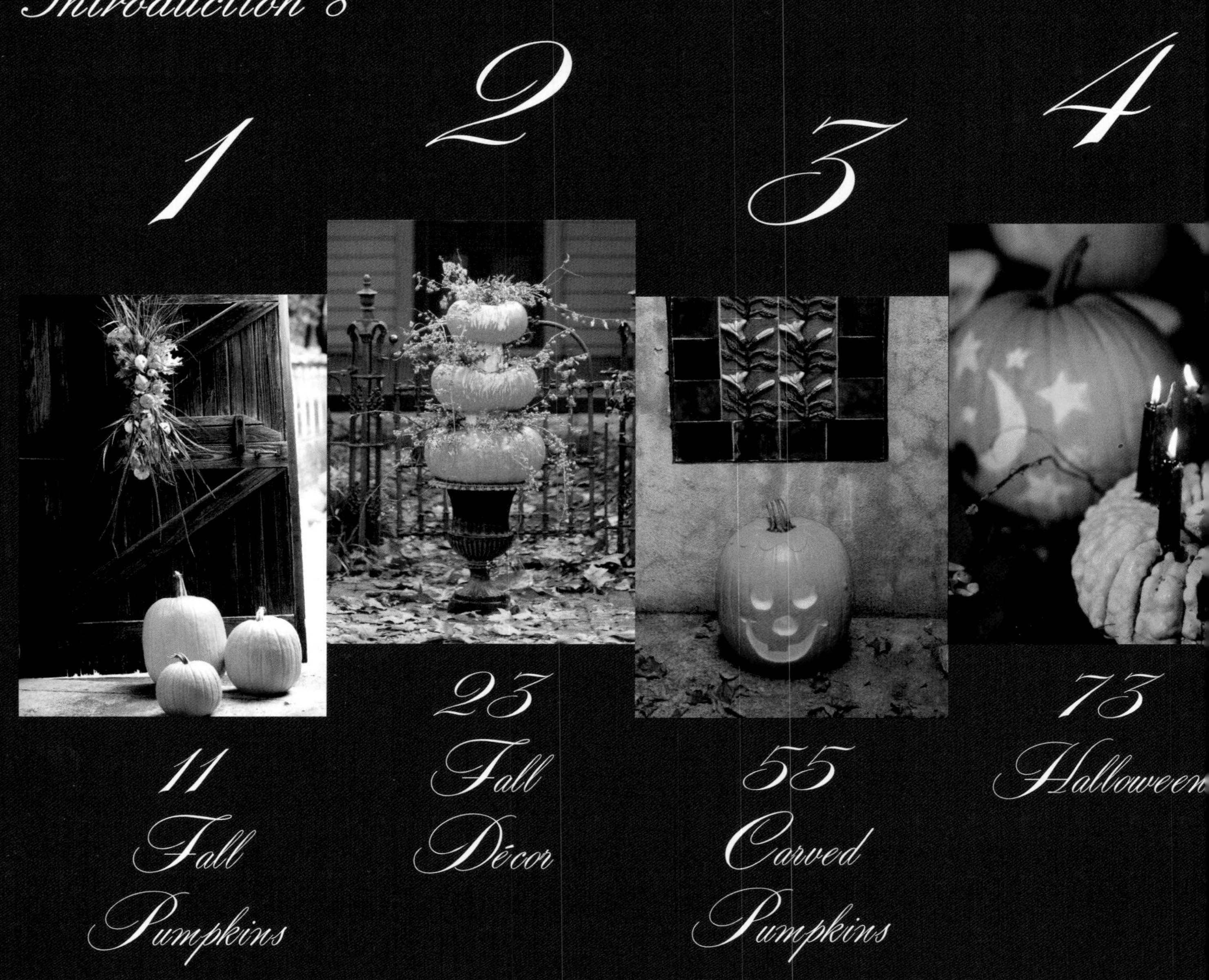

For centuries, pumpkins have been recognized as the symbol of Fall harvest.

The name pumpkin originated from the Greek word for "large melon," "pepon." The English changed the word to "Pumpion" and Shakespeare referred to the "Pumpion" in his work. By the time American colonists harvested their first crop, the name had been transformed to "pumpkin."

A staple of the American Halloween season is the Jack-o'-lantern, a tradition borrowed from Irish folklore where a lost soul named Jack used a hallowed turnip to light his way. The western world adapted the legend when Irish immigrants settled in the United States and found the pumpkin to be a more worthy lantern.

Pumpkin harvest season begins with the first crisp Autumn air and the sounds of children with bright eyes laughing at the sight of colorful pumpkins. The display of pumpkins, as Fall décor, is fashionable through Thanksgiving. While traditional orange pumpkins remain a Fall staple, Heirloom variety pumpkins are gaining in popularity. Harvest time has

never been more gratifying. There are new colors, textures and shapes of pumpkins to create a distinctive Autumn ambiance. In addition, many of the exotic and Heirloom variety pumpkins have astounding culinary qualities, each possessing its own distinctive flavor.

With visual inspiration, your magical Fall journey begins here. Unique pumpkin decorating and culinary tips are shared throughout while stunning images provide a true feast for the eyes. Search no longer for the perfect pumpkin, as you are sure to find it here.

Pumpkins displayed in this book were grown throughout the heartland of America and are readily available at most major food retailers. The Frey-Talley family, based in southeastern Illinois, produced this book simply...

"For The Love of Pumpkins."

Follow Me...

Fall Pumpkins

Chapter 1

How Pumpkins Are Grown and Harvested

Have you ever wondered how pumpkins are grown? Pumpkins and Fall ornamentals are usually planted within the first three weeks of the month of June, when danger of frost has passed and the soil has warmed. The seeds are appropriately spaced to allow vines to spread freely and form canopies that will eventually shade fruit from the hot summer sun. When pumpkin blossoms bloom, nature's pollinators, such as wild honey bees, ensure the successful pollination of the Fall pumpkin crop. Natural rainfall encourages well-developed fruit during the growing season, while shallow cultivation keeps pumpkin patches free of weeds.

As vines commence to lie down and pumpkin fields begin to turn from lush green to speckled orange, attention turns to the Fall harvest. The pumpkins are clipped from their vines and placed by hand into long field rows where they await placement into shipping containers. The containers are loaded onto large trucks and transported to retail stores and roadside markets for families everywhere to enjoy.

This is just the beginning.

Snap Shots

Selecting and Caring for the Perfect Pumpkin

Whether you are selecting your pumpkins at the market or picking them out of a real pumpkin patch, here are some easy tips for finding perfect pumpkins.

Good Jack-o'-lantern carving pumpkins are a Fall decorating staple. They should be harvested once they have fully matured into a deep orange hue. Choose pumpkins that feel firm to the touch and are free of blemishes. Some scarring is unavoidable and is a natural characteristic of real pumpkins. During the growing process, pumpkins tend to lie on their vines as they mature. This causes vine indentations and in some cases minor scarring. Free your pumpkin from the vine by using pruning sheers or a sharp knife. Snapping the stem from the vine may result in a broken or missing "handle." Be sure that you can fit your fingertips around the stem easily. This usually requires between one and two inches of stem length, perfect for a handle. To prevent broken or missing stems avoid carrying your pumpkin by its handle.

Even if you don't plan to carve your pumpkins, select varieties that feel heavy in proportion to size with strong well-attached stems. Pumpkins come in many colors, and it is important when selecting them that they have fully matured into their own unique hue. Be sure that any pumpkin you choose is free from spots of decay. Sometimes these spots can be small white specs that scratch off and reveal darker indentations. It is possible to extend the life of a fresh pumpkin by washing it down with a fruit or vegetable wash. This process removes unwanted pathogens that can cause pumpkins to rapidly decompose.

If you plan to cook your pumpkin, select a variety that can be easily cut and quartered. Preferred varieties of cooking pumpkins are listed in the appendix. During the selection process it is important to consider the size of your cooking pumpkin. One pound of fresh pumpkin typically yields approximately 3/4 cup of pumpkin puree. Most pie recipes with pumpkin usually require between one and two cups of pumpkin puree. Pumpkins for cooking should be stored in a cool dry place at approximately 45-60 degrees.

Striking Orange Pumpkins

Fresh pumpkins pop when placed amidst natural elements. Something so simple makes a bold statement inside or out. Select pumpkins that fit your individual decorating needs. For example, indoors, miniature pumpkins replace summer fruit in this wooden bowl. Meanwhile, large Jack-o'-lantern type pumpkins boldly accent the exterior spaces.

Magical Pumpkins

Throughout this magical Fall journey you will find many interesting pumpkins and gourds with beautiful colors and unique textures. The easiest thing about decorating with live hardy fruit is that its characteristics blend easily with existing natural landscapes. Select a variety of shapes, sizes, colors, and textures to add dimension to any area.

Fall Décor

Chapter

Pumpkin Water Fountain

This beautiful fountain was created using three graduated sizes of Cinderella Pumpkins, carved out as bowls and one Banana Gourd, sectioned into two flat surface pieces. A mixture of bittersweet branches and Fall flowers were used for accents. Water and a small fountain pump were added to the large pumpkin base. The pump hose was attached to the back of the fountain feeding water to the top pumpkin then trickling down.

To create a similar look without water, choose three graduated sizes of pumpkins of a similar shape and stack on top of your favorite urn or planter. Add fresh bittersweet branches and voila you have an amazing, long-lasting Fall sculpture!

Dramatic Fall Table

These beautiful cool toned pumpkins and gourds create a dramatic outdoor table display perfect for an entertaining focal point. To recreate this look, mix designed pumpkins with untouched Heirloom variety pumpkins of similar hues. Hearty Heirloom varieties are long lasting and ideal for etching. The above Jarrahdale pumpkin was etched with the use of a handheld grinder. Easy to use small grinding tools with various sized attachments are available at most local hardware stores. These tools enable you to control the speed and precision of your design. Look ahead to chapter 3 for more carving tips.

Mumkins

The Look

These unique mum-pumpkins lend individual flair to any Fall display. They look excellent in groupings or as a stand alone centerpiece. This look is extremely easy to achieve and mum-pumpkins typicaly last longer than traditionally carved pumpkins.

Create the Look

You will need a pumpkin of any chosen variety, a mum plant, and several color coordinating straight pins. Cut enough mum heads to cover the desired area of your pumpkin, and simply stick one pin through the center of each flower and into the pumpkin. Place them randomly on your pumpkin, or create any desired pattern.

Visions of Fall

Pumpkin Vase

Heirloom variety pumpkins naturally convert into some of the most unique and elegant Autumn vases. The stem end of this vase shaped Heirloom squash was removed and replaced with a fresh Fall floral bouquet. Pheasant feathers were used to accent and provide a traditional harvest appeal. Any selected pumpkin or gourd can be easily transformed into a floral vase or temporary container creating a perfect entertaining focal point. Many examples of pumpkin vases and containers are pictured throughout.

Harvest Swag

Any new or existing swag can be beautifully accented with miniature ornamentals. This pre-fabricated swag was easily transformed into a harvest masterpiece by using floral wire to attach various sizes and varieties of miniature pumpkins and gourds.

Simple Groupings and Placements of Ornamentals

To create a chic Fall look, contrast warm colored ornamentals and cool toned backgrounds (pictured above).

Whimsical Look

The Yellow Rose, a quaint inn nestled in the heart of Indianapolis, Indiana, proved to be a delightful Fall destination. Beautiful pumpkins and ornamentals gave autumn travelers a warm welcome during a cool season. The pie pumpkin placed atop the swan sculpture added a whimsical feel to the Inn's front entrance.

Ornate Settings

Elaborately displayed throughout their long history, Heirloom varieties, have often been showcased in ornate settings. Here a Fairytale pumpkin quietly settles on an enchanting stone fence.

Fall Swag

Fresh miniature pumpkins and gourds adorn this beautiful Fall swag. A simple yet elegant look adds welcoming Autumn warmth to any entrance.

Decorative Corn

Simple and traditional, decorative corn looks great on gates or entrance doors. Select full ears of corn and bundle with floral wire into a group of three. Add a Fall ribbon or leaves to accent.

Pumpkin Style Porch

The soft hue of this Fall display was achieved by using white pumpkins, a Blue Hubbard, and a Marina Di Chioggia Squash. The small hay bales added a seasonal element while the bittersweet branches, dark bat-winged gourds and faux crows provided a brilliant contrast. A ceramic urn with scattered straw created the perfect perch for a curious crow. Easily recreated, this is a great Fall look for traditional porches and entryways.

Mediterranean Fall

Harvest Table

Rustic Harvest Buffet

Create this authentic harvest look by using pie pumpkins, miniature gourds, striped miniature pumpkins, seasonal berries and Fall flowers.

Carved Pumpkins

Chapter 3

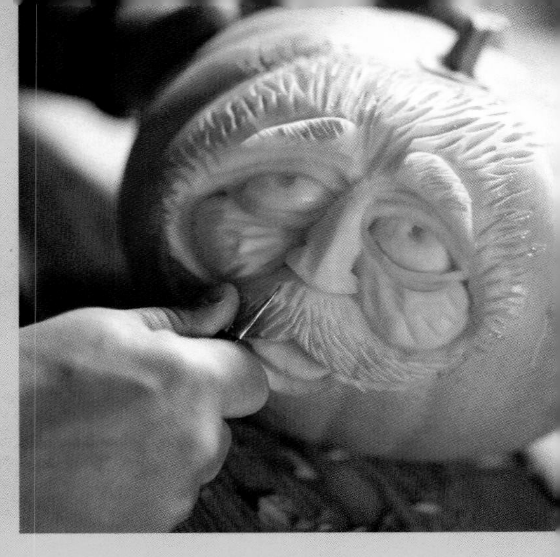

Carving Pumpkins

Whether you are an amateur carver or a professional, pumpkins offer some of the most unique canvases for you to create a masterpiece. Dimensions are easily achieved due to the differences in exterior and interior surface colors. Pumpkin texture also makes free-hand whittling a breeze due to the supple carving surface. Meatier Heirloom varieties such as those shown are best for this type of look.

Select carving tools that you feel comfortable in maneuvering. Power equipment may be used as well. A nontoxic spray enamel may be used to preserve carvings.

Carving Hard Shell Gourds

Hard shell gourds have had quite an evolution. Their uses include: dishes, ladles, drinking cups, bird houses and so much more. They can be harvested when green and then quietly allowed to go through a natural decaying process which leaves the interior shell in tact. The interior shell can then be cleaned by using warm water and a scouring pad. Once clean and dry you have yet another beautiful canvas. We love them painted, stained, carved, burned or all of the above.

Etchings

Here a small power grinding tool is used to perform surface etchings. This quick and efficient precision technique is simple to master on gourds or pumpkins.

BOO

BOO!

Halloween at the Orchard House

The Orchard House, located in New Harmony, Indiana, lends itself as the ideal backdrop for this luminous grouping of carved pumpkins. At this charming destination, guests were greeted with traditionally carved Jack-o'-lanterns accented by a few white pumpkins. Stalks embellished with ears of decorative corn assisted in establishing a natural Fall environment. This is a classic way to invite trick-or-treaters or simply family and friends. Basic faces and designs look best when arranging several carvings. When creating this look, remember to mix it up a bit with various sizes of pumpkins and a few that are not carved. Battery operated mini lights are recommended to provide safer illumination.

Relief Carvings

There are many different techniques to choose from when you plan to carve your pumpkin. Pumpkins come in many colors and sizes. The green pumpkin on the right was carved by using the relief technique. This technique enables you to create an image by simply carving away the background surface. A beautiful Fall leaf appears as the surface of green was removed. The inside of the leaf was carved in the same way to give a 3-D appearance. Generally, this style of carving will last longer than traditional methods. Applying non-toxic clear finish will extend the life of the pumpkin and maintain the integrity of your design. Wood carving tools were used to achieve this impression. Various pumpkin carving tools are available at major retail stores.

Traditional Carvings

Carving Jack-o-lanterns can create fond and memorable experiences for the entire family. A process that is so simple can produce unforgettable results.

You will need:

I carving pumpkin
I large boning knife
I small paring knife
I large spoon or ice cream scoop
I large bowl
A dry-erase marker or pencil
Old newspaper
Several paper towels

Use the pencil or marker to outline a circle around the pumpkin's stem. This will be the Jack-o'-lantern's lid. You may prefer to cut a lid from the bottom rather than the top, since this can make it easier to replace and light candles.

Cut along the line using the boning knife. Point the knife inward (toward the center of the pumpkin) at about a 45-degree angle.

Remove the pulp from the pumpkin using the ice cream scoop or your hands. Children can safely be involved in this part of the process. Scrape the internal meat of the pumpkin away from the area you plan to carve leaving approximately one inch behind. Place the pulp in the bowl if you plan to roast the pumpkin seeds later.

Sketch the Jack-o'-lantern's face on the surface of the pumpkin. Use a paring knife to cut along the outline of your design. Place a candle or mini light in the base of the pumpkin to illuminate.

Pumpkin Glow

Candle-lit, carved pumpkins are a great way to create a warm ambiance around the fireplace. If you are anxious to get that wood burning fireplace going, but it just isn't quite cold enough, try this beautiful room warming technique. Arrange carved pumpkins at varying heights using metal or non-flamable props.

Halloween

Chapter 4

Perfect Pumpkin Party Accents

Suspending pumpkins and ornamentals is a unique way to captivate party guests. Used as hanging lanterns, these can be customized to illuminate any area.

You will need:

Several mini pumpkins and gourds
Carving tools
Small scoop
Floral wire or twine
Battery operated miniature lights
Optional drill

Cut tops of mini pumpkins and gourds into lids and scoop out seeds. Carve faces or designs. Drill two holes in the side of pumpkin or gourd. Thread wire or twine through each hole and tie off into a knot inside. Place tea light or small battery bulb in each lantern. Do not use tea lights with twine. Replace lid and hang.

Pumpkin Candelabra

Heirloom variety pumpkins make sturdy long lasting candelabras (pictured left). They can be used as the focal point or a unique party accent. Use black candle tapers for dramatic Halloween displays or warm tones for a Fall harvest look.

Select your Heirloom pumpkin. Drill or carve six symmetrical holes the size of your taper ends on top of pumpkin. Finally insert six candle tapers.

Pumpkin Party Brain Game Recipe

1 large Jack-o'-lantern pumpkin
1 or 2 boxes of spaghetti noodles
2 packs candy worms
Several plastic creepy crawly prizes

Cook noodles according to package instructions. Cut top off of pumpkin and loosen seeds inside. You may leave the seeds and pulp for extra goo. Add spaghetti noodles and all additional ingredients. Mix well by using hands.

Pumpkin Treat Holders

Set your party table with these autumn pie pumpkin treat holders. Use a small drill bit to make evenly spaced holes in the pumpkin. Then simply place a sucker in each hole to create a one of a kind treat display.

Pumpkin Pots

Pie pumpkins are the perfect size for individual treat pots. To make simply cut off the top of a small pumpkin and scoop out the seeds. Line with material of choice and fill with treats. If you want to go a step further, attach a handle to make a treat bucket. This will require a drill and either twine, wire, or plastic tie.

TRICK

Hanging Pie Pumpkins

Staggering in height, hanging pumpkins dangle like chimes during the Fall season. This is an unforgettable way to deck the Fall with fresh pumpkins! Create a symmetrical look by choosing pumpkin varieties of similar shapes, color, and size.

You will need:

Pie pumpkins
Light gauge wire
Power drill with small bit

Choose pumpkins with sturdy handles. Carefully drill a small hole horizontally through the stem. Cut wire the appropriate hanging length and thread one end through the stem. Tie the threaded wire off into a sturdy knot at the stem end. Finally, hang your dangling pumpkins from a sturdy eye hook or planter hanger.

B
O
O

Green Witch Pumpkin

You will need:

Large Jack-o'-lantern pumpkin
Warty ornamental gourd (nose)
Egg shaped gourd cut in half (eyes)
Raffia
Witch's hat
White paint pen
Black paint pen
Green paint
Toothpicks

Cut off the base section of a warty ornamental gourd. The gourd should then fit flush on the large Jack-o'-lantern pumpkin. Properly align the gourd to the nose position and attach to the large pumpkin with toothpicks (you may also use putty or glue). This will create the warty nose. Paint the gourd and pumpkin with green acrylic paint and let dry. Cut a white egg shaped gourd in half to create eyes. Paint on details of the eye ball with black and green paint markers. Attach to painted pumpkin with your choice of adhesives previously listed. Use paint pens or acrylic paint to create the mouth. Top off the witch with raffia like hair and a witch's hat.

Monster Punkies

These friendly monsters are a kid favorite. Big imaginations easily transform the unique textures of ornamental gourds and miniature pumpkins into cool creatures.

You will need:

Assorted miniature pumpkins and gourds
Neon non-toxic acrylic paints (assorted colors)
Paint brush
Wiggle eyes
Pipe cleaners
Colored feathers
Non-toxic white glue

Bring your Monster Punkies to life by painting them entirely with bright neon or glow in the dark paints. Once figures dry, facial features and artistic patterns can be added. Finish by gluing on accents such as wiggle eyes, feathers, and pipe cleaners.

Pumpkin Games

Chapter

Pumpkin Putt

Transform any backyard into a pumpkin golf outing. This fun party game keeps both children and adults entertained for hours. Painted and carved pumpkins set the mood for an all out Fall fun fest.

These colorful friendly faces and scenes were painted with paint pens allowing greater design control. To save time you can purchase hand painted pumpkins in advance at most major retailers. General carving tools were used to create the pumpkin course obstacles. To construct the decorative pumpkin totem pole, a metal fence post was used as an armature to support the painted pumpkins that were carefully tilted and slid down on top of each other. Several painted pumpkins were needed to cover the post.

Pumpkin Toss

5

3
4
5

Pumpkin Toss

This classic game takes on a Fall twist when using fresh pumpkins. Simple to set up and perfect for all ages, Pumpkin Toss is sure to be a party game favorite.

You will need:

Several miniature pumpkins
5 graduated sized Jack-o'-lanterns
Carving tools
Black paint pen

Cut and remove the tops of the five Jack-o'-lanterns and scoop out the insides. Place the pumpkins in a row from smallest to largest. Number them from one to five using a paint pen. Have the children stand behind a line taking turns tossing miniature pumpkins into the Jack-o'-lanterns in number order. When he or she misses a pumpkin, it is the next child's turn.

Pumpkin Piñata

Pumpkin Piñata

Celebrate Fall with a festive Autumn Piñata.

You will need:

I large Jack-o'-lantern pumpkin
Rope
Carving tools and drill
Optional paint pens

Select a large pumpkin. Use a carving tool or paint pens to apply designs to your pumpkin. Cut the top out of the pumpkin and remove seeds. Carefully scrape meat away inside of the pumpkin to create a thin shell that is easily breakable. This usually requires less than one half inch of pumpkin thickness. Drill two symmetrical holes into the top of the pumpkin, and then drill two more matching holes in the base. Thread the rope through the eye holes supporting the base and fill with candy. Thread the rope ends back through the top. Securely suspend and swing away.

Pumpkin Checkers

Pumpkin Checkers

Miniature pumpkins settle on a burlap checker board for some Fall fun. A traditional game suddenly becomes new and exciting when bright pumpkins fill the board. You can make your own pumpkin checker board or purchase a large manufactured one. In either case be sure the square sizes are at least 5x5 inches. Let the games begin!

You will need:

12 white mini pumpkins
12 orange mini pumpkins
1½ square yard of burlap
1 can of black spray paint
32 5x5 inch pieces of contact paper

Place the burlap flat and arrange the 32 pieces of contact paper in an 8x8 checkered grid. Spray paint the burlap. When the paint has dried, remove the contact paper to uncover the handcrafted checker board. Use orange and white mini pumpkins as game pieces.

Thanksgiving

Chapter 6

Homemade Pumpkin Pie

INGREDIENTS:

- I ¼ cups fresh pumpkin puree
- ¾ cup sugar
- ½ teaspoon salt
- ¼ teaspoon ground ginger
- I teaspoon ground cinnamon
- I teaspoon all-purpose flour
- ¼ teaspoon nutmeg
- 2 eggs, lightly beaten
- I cup evaporated milk, undiluted
- I table tablespoon rum (optional)
- 2 tablespoons water
- ½ teaspoon vanilla extract
- I unbaked pastry shell (9-inch)

PREPARATION:

Combine pumpkin, sugar, salt, spices, nutmeg, and flour in a medium mixing bowl. Add eggs; mix well. Add evaporated milk, water, rum, and vanilla; mix well. Pour into pastry-lined pie pan. Bake at 400° for 15 minutes; reduce heat to 350° and bake about 35 minutes longer, or until center is set.

Homemade Whipped Cream

I pie = I cup of whipping cream

½ cup heavy cream
½ cup confectioners' sugar
½ teaspoon vanilla extract

Combine all ingredints and blend with electric mixer set to high speed. Cream is ready when soft peaks have formed.

Preparing Fresh Pumpkin Puree

1. Slice selected pumpkin in half and clean out seeds and pulp.
2. Place halves face down in a baking dish. Bake at 325 degrees F for 45-50 minutes.
3. Let cool and then peel outer skin. Cube pumpkin flesh and reduce to pulp in blender, food processor or with a potato masher.

Pumpkin Bread

INGREDIENTS

- 2 cups flour
- 1 teaspoon baking soda
- 1 teaspoon salt
- 1 teaspoon pumpkin pie spice
- 1 ½ cups sugar
- ½ cup vegetable oil
- 2 eggs beaten
- 1 cup cooked pumpkin
- ¼ cup water
- ¼ cup finely chopped nuts (optional)

DIRECTIONS

1. Sift dry ingredients together.
2. Blend sugar, oil, eggs, pumpkin and water and add to flour mixture. Blend well. Fold in nuts.
3. Pour into greased, floured 9x5" loaf pan and bake at 350 degrees F for 1 hour.

Easy Pumpkin Butter

INGREDIENTS

- ½ cup softened butter
- ¼ cup honey
- ¼ cup pumpkin puree
- 1/8 teaspoon pumpkin spice

DIRECTIONS

Combine all ingredients and whip until smooth.

Frosted Pumpkin Bars

INGREDIENTS

- 2 cups flour
- 2 teaspoons cinnamon
- 1 pinch of ground cloves
- 1 teaspoon baking soda
- 1 teaspoon baking powder
- ½ teaspoon salt
- 2 cups sugar
- 1 cup salad oil
- 4 eggs, beaten
- 1 cup cooked pumpkin
- 1 cup chopped pecans

INGREDIENTS (Frosting)

- 1 (8oz) package softened cream cheese
- ½ cup softened butter
- 1 teaspoon milk
- 1 teaspoon vanilla
- 1 (16oz) box confectioners' sugar

DIRECTIONS

1. Combine flour, spices and salt. In a separate bowl mix sugar, oil, eggs and pumpkin.
2. Stir flour mixture into pumpkin mixture and beat well.
3. Fold in chopped pecans.
4. Pour into greased 9x13" cake pan. Bake at 325 degrees F for 20 minutes.
5. Mix all ingredients for frosting and coat bars once cooled.

Pumpkin Rum Sauce

INGREDIENTS

- 2 egg yolks
- 1 shot of Rum
- 1 cup confectioners' sugar
- 1 pich of pumpkin spice
- 1 cup of heavy whipping cream
- 1 teaspoon vanilla extract

DIRECTIONS

1. Beat egg yolks and rum. Add to sugar and spice. Mix well.
2. Whip cream and vanilla untill stiff and fold into mixture.

Pour over favorite pumpkin dish or poached fruit. Pumpkin rum is an excellent topping over ice cream and pumpkin pie.

Roasted Pumpkin Seeds

1. Rinse pumpkin seeds under cold water and pick out the pulp and strings. Place the pumpkin seeds in a single layer on an oiled baking sheet, stirring to coat. If you prefer, omit the oil and coat with non-stick cooking spray.
2. Sprinkle with salt; bake at 325 degrees F until toasted, about 25 minutes, checking and stirring after 10 minutes.
3. Let cool and store in an air-tight container.

Pumpkin Soup

INGREDIENTS

- 6 cups chicken stock
- 1 ½ teaspoons salt
- 4 cups pumpkin puree
- ¼ teaspoon ground nutmeg
- 1 cup chopped onion
- 1 teaspoon chopped fresh thyme
- 1 clove garlic, minced
- 10 whole black peppercorns
- ½ cup heavy whipping cream
- ½ teaspoon hot sauce
- ½ cup Swiss cheese
- ½ breadcrumbs
- 1 teaspoon chopped fresh parsley

DIRECTIONS

1. Heat stock, salt, pumpkin, onion, thyme, garlic, nutmeg, and peppercorns. Bring to a boil, reduce heat to low, and simmer for 30 minutes uncovered.
2. Allow soup to cool and then puree using a food processor or blender.
3. Return to pan, and bring to a boil again. Reduce heat to low, and simmer for another 30 minutes, uncovered. Stir in heavy cream, hot sauce, cheese and bread crumbs. Pour into soup bowls and garnish with fresh parsley or roasted pumpkin seeds.

Pumpkin Roll

INGREDIENTS

- 3 eggs
- 1 cup white sugar
- 2/3 cup solid pack pumpkin puree
- 1 teaspoon lemon juice
- ¾ cup sifted all-purpose flour
- 1 teaspoon baking powder
- ½ teaspoon salt
- 2 teaspoons ground cinnamon
- 1 teaspoon ground ginger
- 1 cup chopped pecans
- 1 (8 oz) package cream cheese
- 4 tablespoons butter
- 1 cup confectioners' sugar
- ½ teaspoon vanilla extract
- ½ oz grated chocolate (white or dark)
- confectioners' sugar for dusting

DIRECTIONS

1. Preheat oven to 350 degrees F. Grease and flour a 10x15 inch jellyroll pan.
2. In a large bowl, beat eggs and sugar with an electric mixer on high speed for five minutes. Gradually mix in pumpkin and lemon juice. Combine the flour, baking powder, salt, cinnamon, and ginger; stir into the pumpkin mixture. Spread batter evenly into the prepared pan. Sprinkle pecans over the top of the batter.
3. Bake for 12-15 minutes, or until the center springs back when touched. Loosen edges with a knife. Turn out on a flat pillowcase that has been dusted with confectioners' sugar. Roll up cake using pillowcase, and let cool for about 20 minutes.
4. In a medium bowl, combine cream cheese, butter, 1 cup confectioners' sugar, grated chocolate and vanilla. Beat until smooth. Unroll pumpkin cake when cool, spread with filling, and roll up. Place pumpkin roll on a long sheet of waxed paper, and dust with confectioners' sugar. Wrap cake in waxed paper, and twist ends of waxed paper like a candy wrapper. Refrigerate overnight. Serve chilled; before slicing, dust with additional confectioners' sugar.

Children's Thanksgiving Table

Make your little pilgrim guests feel special with their very own harvest table. Fun craft activities keep children entertained on Thanksgiving day while the real turkey roasts. These easy to make Tiny Turkeys and colorful button pumpkins brighten any children's table. Thanksgiving has never been so fun!

Tiny Turkey

You will need:

Miniature pumpkin
Brown paint
Red paint
Yellow paint
Sheet of red foam
Wiggle eyes
Craft sticks
School glue
Paint brush and scissors

How to:

Paint your miniature pumpkin brown and the stem yellow. While the pumpkin is drying, paint two craft sticks red, two yellow, and mix the red and yellow paint to make one orange. Cut out a head and gobbler out of the red foam. The size of the turkey head will depend on the size of the pumpkin you are using. Cut a slit in the foam to slide over the stem and glue on wiggle eyes. Flip over and glue on painted craft sticks in a fan shape.

Pumpkin Totem Pole

This whimsical Thanksgiving accent brightens up any harvest table. Children are sure to love the bright colored harvest faces. This look is easy to achieve and little ones can even help.

You will need:

5 miniature pumpkins
1 pie pumpkin
1 dowel rod cut to desired size
Assorted colored paint pens
or miniature pumpkin face tattoos
Drill
Pencil sharpener

This pumpkin totem pole was created with one pie pumpkin and five miniature pumpkins. Imaginative faces were painted on each pumpkin with paint markers and pumpkin tattoos. A wooden dowel rod was sharpened in a pencil sharpener and punched into the larger pie pumpkin at stem end providing the base. Offset holes were then drilled into the miniature pumpkins. They were then threaded over the dowel rod.

Button Pumpkins

Spare buttons come in handy on Thanksgiving. Spice up a colorful Heirloom pumpkin with unique buttons. This quick and easy project is a must for a fun Fall table. Simply embellish your pumpkin with randomly placed colorful buttons. Use a low temperature hot glue gun or school glue to attach the buttons. Be resourceful and have fun! Keep child safety in mind when displaying this Button Pumpkin as buttons may be easily removed.

Chapter 7
Fall Weddings & Events

White Pearl Wedding Pumpkins

White pumpkins sparkle at a Fall Wedding. Personalized with calligraphy and embellished with sophisticated pearl pins, these posh pumpkins are sure to have guests beaming with delight.

• • • • • • • • • • • • •

You will need:

- White pumpkin
- Pearl pins
- White glue
- White glitter
- Sponge brush
- Black paint pen

Dilute the white glue with water and paint onto the pumpkin using sponge brush. Sprinkle white glitter over the wet glue surface and let dry. Insert pearl pins into the pumpkin at random or in a pattern. Flowers can be added using the same technique as "Mumkins".

Justin
Sarah

Justin
Sarah

Personalized Pumpkins

Fall occasions are the perfect time to greet and identify guests with personalized pumpkins and place settings. Inscribe names by printing calligraphy directly on the pumpkins or saw grooves into the stems and attach personalized cards.

Frontier Community
College

Tamaroa Grade
School

Autumn Elegance

A Jarrahdale pumpkin overflows in abundant floral elegance, lending a unique Autumn accent to a beautifully decorated table. Achieve this look with your favorite Heirloom pumpkin and a fresh array of floral accents.

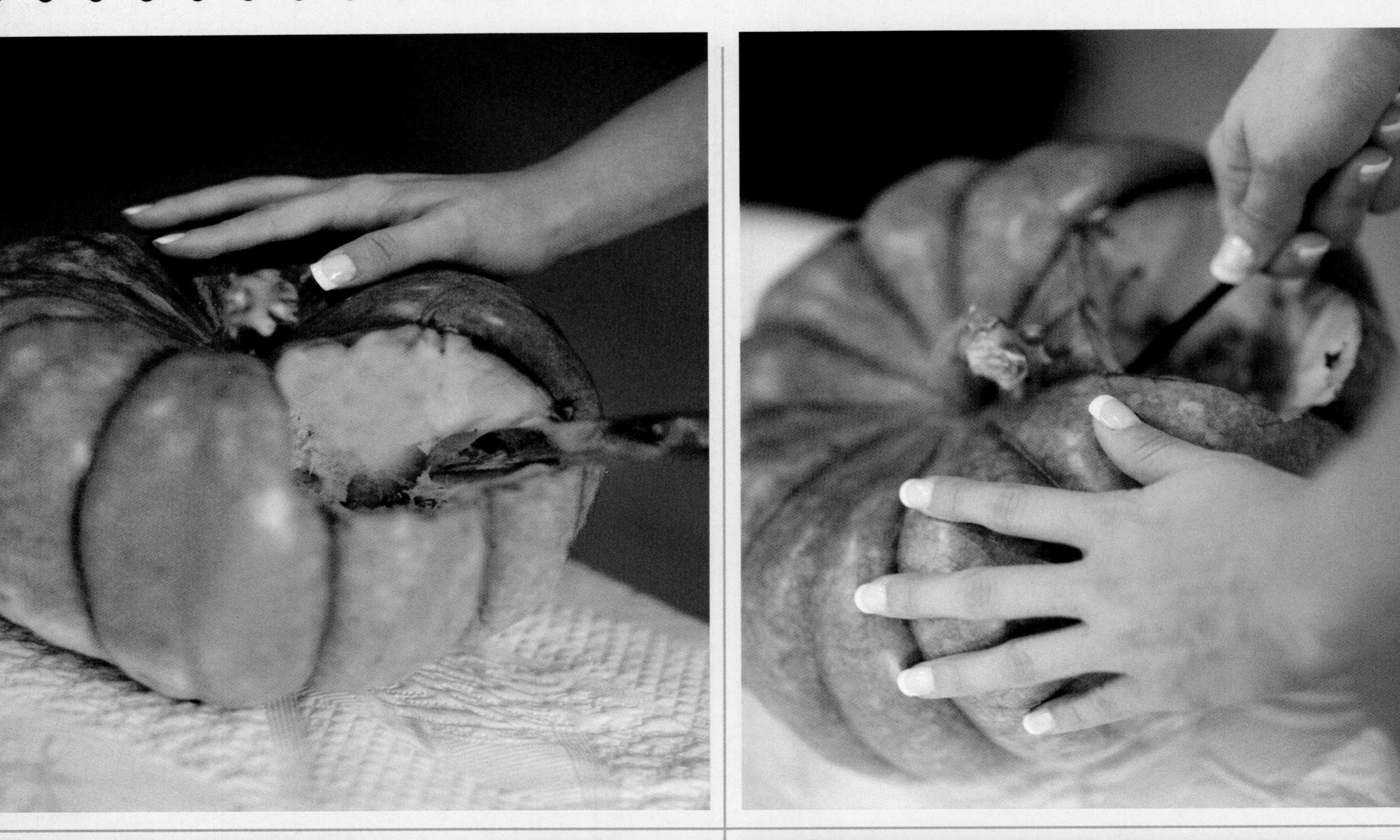

Harvest Toast

Long stemmed crystal champaign glasses gleam amongst pretty orange miniature pumpkins. The head table of this bridal event was elegantly adorned with Fall ornamentals and harvest colors.

Pumpkin Garnish

Garnish any Fall cake or food item with shimmering miniature pumpkins. For an edible alternative to glitter pumpkins use ordinary sugar to make your pumpkins sparkle. First, paint your pumpkins with a tacky substance such as clear corn syrup and then sprinkle on a coat of white sugar. Both miniature pumpkins and ornamental gourds make delightful Fall garnishes.

Contemporary Cornucopia

A traditional wicker harvest Cornucopia is given a contemporary edge when spray painted with black acrylic paint. Natural white miniature pumpkins and gourds overflow in abundance creating a fresh Fall look.

White Pumpkin Wedding

I went to a white pumpkin wedding today
The loveliest I've ever seen
Everywhere that I looked a beautiful sight
Flowers in pumpkins so clean and so bright
Tables decorated in candle light
Such a lovely Fall setting for their special night
Put together by few for the many to see
A white pumpkin wedding for my beau and me.

Diana Rae Waterstradt

Groom's Pumpkin Party

A painted pumpkin bridal party is a creative addition to the traditional groom's cake. Perfect for Fall weddings this group is easily created by drawing simple doodles on pumpkins and then filling in with colors. Embellish your painted pumpkins with a top hat, veil, and flowers. Personalized, they make great bridal party gifts. Once your bridesmaids and groomsmen have enjoyed their pumpkin for the season, the seeds can then be saved and planted in the Bride and Groom's honor the following spring.

Autumn Amoré

Appendix

Chapter

Jack-o'-lantern Pumpkin

True and timeless, the traditional Jack-o'-lantern Pumpkin symbolizes Fall and harvest time. Predominately orange but varying in sizes, the Jack-o'-lantern pumpkin is a Fall decorating basic. There are thousands of uses for the Jack-o'-lantern, but the most familiar is carving. Rarely is the use of the Jack-o'-lantern pumpkin recommended for culinary purposes, however the seeds are good for baking.

Blue Hubbard Squash

The Blue Hubbard Squash is an old time favorite. This variety of winter squash has bright orange, fine textured flesh which is quite sweet. The Hubbard is widely noted for its excellent storing quality through the winter months and is delicious in pies or cut into serving size pieces and baked or steamed. Try savory mashed squash as a seasonal alternative to potatoes as a side dish! The Hubbard is also a great Fall decorating basic (See page 37).

Jarrahdale Pumpkin

The Jarrahdale Pumpkin is a flattened grayish-blue string-less variety from Australia. Its defining coloration and unusual shape will enhance your Fall displays until you're ready to bake it into a pie. The thick deep orange flesh of the Jarrahdale Pumpkin is rich in flavor and is a preferred culinary pumpkin. The Jarrahdale Pumpkin also provides a wonderful canvas for surface carvings. Once carved, there is a brilliant contrast between the greyish-blue skin and the orange flesh (See page 59).

Cinderella Pumpkin

Also known as Rouge Vif d'Estampess, the Cinderella Pumpkin, was introduced to the US in the late 1800's. Its shape and color is reminiscent of Cinderella's carriage. It has a thick yet tender deep orange flesh full of flavor. Excellent for décor and culinary purposes this timeless pumpkin is a Fall must-have (See page 25).

One Too Many Pumpkin

This delightful pumpkin looks as if it has had a late night, hence the name One Too Many. Although a relatively new variety of pumpkin, One Too Many has become one of the most sought after pumpkins on the market. Its unique coloring and texture is anything but predictable when it comes to Fall décor. Although it may be used for culinary purposes, this pumpkin is most likely to appear in Fall displays.

White Pumpkin

The White Pumpkin, commonly referred to as ghost pumpkin, is medium-sized and lightly ribbed with bright orange flesh. Meatier vairietes of white pumpkins are great for cooking and baking while varieties that resemble the traditional Jack-o'-lantern are better for carving. White Pumpkins are a great way to create an up-to-date Fall look. After the Fall season is over White Pumpkins can easily be converted into a whimsical snowmen.

Buckskin Pumpkin

The Autumn Buckskin Pumpkin is a sizeable tan pumpkin with natural patina. It is great for baking and lends itself as a beautiful decorating element for natural Fall displays. A Frey Farms favorite, the Autumn Buckskin is a mainstay in soups and casseroles during the harvest season. It is also one of the preferred canning pumpkins.

Pie Pumpkin

Traditional Pie Pumpkins are classic orange in color. Sizing is usually consistent while the flesh is tender and flavorful. Pie Pumpkins are a Fall decorating staple and can easily be converted into your favorite pumpkin dish. Storing pumpkins in a cool dry place, approximately 45 to 60 degrees Fahrenheit, will extend their lives long into the winter months (See page 85-87).

Banana Squash

This long banana shaped squash is pinkish in color and has a delicious yellow-orange flesh. They can grow up to 50 lbs and can be used in any Fall display. The Banana Squash is also a magnificent cooking squash that offers a creamy texture with a fruity, buttery flavor. This squash was used in the Pumpkin Fountain featured on page 25.

Red Warty Thing Pumpkin

Bursting with bold color and bumpy texture, Red Warty Thing is an unusual addition to Fall decorating. The thick hearty rind protects its Hubbard type flesh from natural elements. While it may be used for culinary purposes, this pumpkin will most likely be chosen for its aesthetic appeal. The uniqueness of the Red Warty Thing pumpkin is sure to have friends and neighbors talking.

Marina di Chioggia

This large, turban-shaped fruit is known as the sea pumpkin of Chioggia, Italy, a costal town south of Venice. Deep blue-green in color and bumpy in texture, the Marina di Chioggia is one of the most beautiful and unique of all squash. Its rich, sweet flesh is a deep yellow-orange that is of good quality and delicious baked or in pies. These stunning fruit generally weigh about 10 lbs and are produced on vigorous vines.

Peanut Pumpkin

Also know as Galeux d'Eysines, the Peanut Pumpkin is a French Heirloom variety pumpkin. This flattened, round fruit has a gorgeous salmon to peach colored skin which is covered with peanut-like warts! The Peanut Pumpkin is perhaps one of the most interesting squash varieties that you will ever see! The sweet orange flesh is used in France for soups and can also be baked. For decorating purposes the Peanut Pumpkin makes a great alien or spooky candelabra.

Miniature Gourds

Festive mixes of Miniature Gourds are a harvest time decorating staple. Gourds are natural pieces of Fall décor that come in many different shapes, colors and textures. Potential decorating uses are unlimited and each piece provides a unique canvas for the Fall decorator.

White Mini Gourds

These miniature white treasures are usually found mixed with a regular assortment of Miniature Gourds. Some varieties such as the egg gourd mature to a creamy white tint while others are special finds. Due to their elegance, decorating with White Minature Gourds has become a growing trend.

Miniature White Pumpkin

Brilliant white miniature pumpkins are a decorator's dream. Many homes are decorated with white accents so naturally white miniature pumpkins bring the perfect Fall element indoors. Whether displayed in an exotic Mediterranean location or a traditional Autumn setting, Miniature White Pumpkins update any harvest look.

Mini Striped Pumpkins

Circus-like striped miniature pumpkins make great little conversation pieces. Groupings of striped pumpkins pop when placed in the midst of cool blue backgrounds. These fun miniatures have recently begun to appear in supermarkets and roadside stands across the nation.

Turk's Turban

This bright orange, squash-type gourd with red, white, and dark green markings, also known as the Mexican hat, is excellent for baking and stuffing. From a decorating standpoint, Turbans can be easily converted into funky aliens or other holiday creatures. Naturally, the bright colors of "Turks Turban" aide in defining any Fall display.

Orange Striped Cushaw

This oblong shaped squash displays firm white skin with distinctive golden to tan stripes. These unique markings lend character to any Fall décor. The Cushaw is renowned for its culinary qualities... this IS the one your Grandmother used in her famous pie recipe.

Crooked Neck Squash

Also known as a neck pumpkin the Crooked Neck Squash is an Heirloom form of Butternut squash. The long solid curving neck can reach almost two feet in size. Bright orange and sweet inside, only the meaty neck is needed to make many of your favorite pumpkin dishes. The seeds are located in the bulb cavity so there is no need to scrape them away. Simply cut off the neck and cook.

Orange Mini Pumpkins

Adorable Orange Miniature Pumpkins have become a Fall classic. An all time kids favorite, these Orange Miniature Pumpkins brighten up workspace for big kids as well. They are perfect for indoor or outdoor use, and the crafting potential for this or any miniature pumpkin is endless. Miniature pumpkins were used to create Tiny Turkeys featured on page 116.

Hard-shell Gourds

Hard-shell Gourds are named after their thick skin and grow in various shapes and sizes. Their popularity dates back to pre-historic times when uses included kitchen utensils, tools, fishing floats, whistles, rattles and musical instruments of every kind. Once allowed to go through the natural decaying process, gourds may be decorated by using techniques such as wood burning, carving, dying and painting (See page 60).

Fairytale Pumpkin

Musquee de Provence also know as Fairytale Pumpkin is a unique eating and ornamental pumpkin. The dense flesh is delicious for baking. During the growing process, dark green and peach colored blushes appear. Once mature, this heavily ridged French Heirloom variety pumpkin turns a buff orange color. This variety is also known for its excellent storage potential.

Giant Pumpkins

Generally viewed as a Fall novelty item, giant pumpkins grow in a variety of shapes, sizes and colors. The World of Color variety, pictured here, is a colorful mixture of Giant Pumpkins. They are used for pumpkin competition weigh-offs and surface at harvest festivals around the world. Fond memories are often created when families grow giant pumpkins together.

Pumpkin Water Fountain

(pp. 23-25)

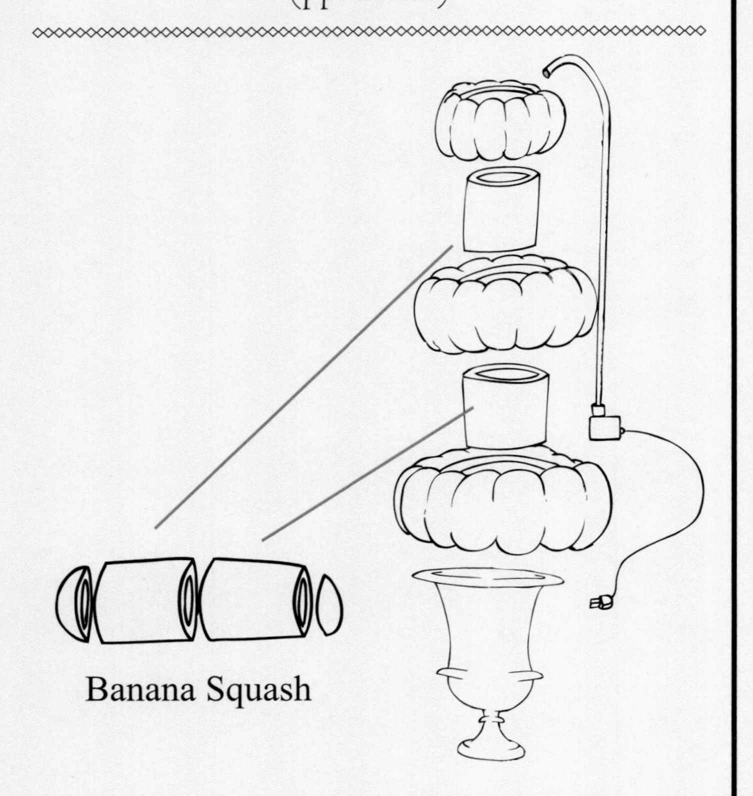

Tiny Turkey

(pp. 116-117)

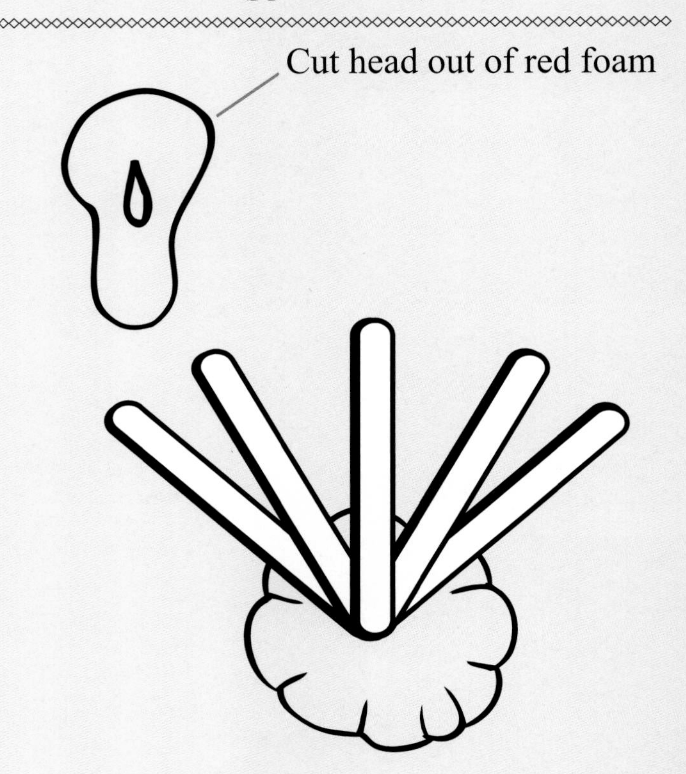

Pumpkin Piñata

(pp. 102-103)

Pumpkin Putt

(pp. 94-97)

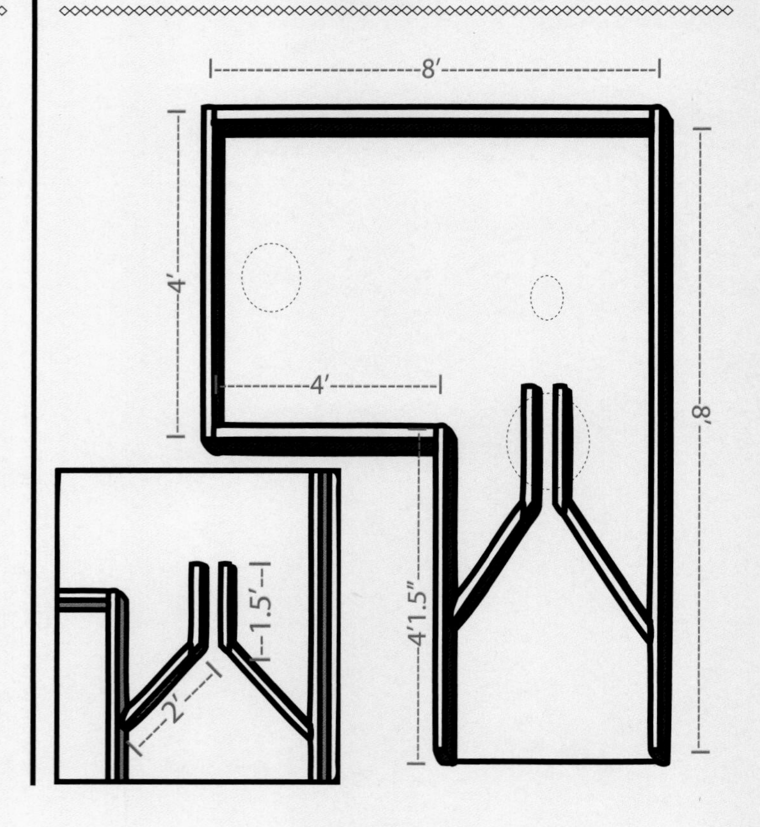

Sarah Marie Talley

As the president and CEO of Frey Farms, a family operated business; Sarah Marie Frey-Talley is dedicated to bringing the small, local farmer approach to the production and marketing of fresh produce. Selling melons to local grocery stores at the age of eight was just the beginning of her love of the produce business. Her passion for pumpkins and Fall ornamentals is clearly illustrated throughout "FOR THE LOVE OF *Pumpkins*". Fully engaged in the produce industry, Sarah is the President of the newly founded "National Pumpkin Growers Association" and serves on many industry boards. Her commitment to the produce industry has earned her and her companies several industry awards. In 2006 she was named the Frontier College "Alumnus of the Year" and was recently honored by Produce Business magazine as one of the produce industry's top "40-Under Forty" leaders. In 2005 the Harvard School of Business conducted a case study regarding her business techniques and negotiation strategies. Surrounded by people she loves, Sarah contributes both her personal and professional success to her supportive family. She lives in Southern Illinois on her family farm with her husband Justin and two growing sons William and Luke.

Angela R. Talley

A photographer renowned for her ability to utilize natural lighting resulting in sensitive interpretations, Angela R. Talley is one of the most distinguished photographers in the nation. From her technical mastery evolves artistic expression in image. Her photographs are works of art in both composition and mood. Angela's passion is found through the lens of a camera. While the diversity of her portfolio is intentional, she maintains a definitive style. Her work encompasses a broad spectrum from lifestyle, weddings, family, and editorial photography. Angela lives in Indianapolis, Indiana with her husband Chris and two daughters Journie and Lucia. Her work is profiled at angelatalley.com.

Special Thanks

Special thanks to Red Geranium Enterprises and Mrs. Jane Blaffer Owen for graciously welcoming us into their properties and providing accommodations to the Frey Farms team during the creation of this book. The peaceful town of New Harmony, Indiana, a writer's sanctuary, is filled with the kindest and most artistically gifted people that I have ever met. One hundred and twenty-five acres of gardens, fountains, ponds and sculptures located at the New Harmony Inn provided the most stunning backdrops for our pumpkins. For peace and creative inspiration, I highly recommend a stay at any of the glorious Red Geranium properties in New Harmony, Indiana.

On behalf of the entire Frey-Talley family I would like to thank the following people for the dedication and creative inspriation they contributed during the creation of this book, notably: John Frey, Andrea Frey, Anna Frey, Leonard Frey, Aidan Frey, Wendy Turner, Lillian Manning, Ted Frey, Grace Frey, Rebecca Whede, Harley Frey, Justin Talley, William Talley, Luke Talley, Elizabeth Reitz, Angela Martin, Journie Talley, Chris Talley, Bob Talley, Trish Talley, Gearry Davenport, Katie Harvey, Judith Ann Harvey, Betty Davis, Judy Stallings, Tonya Kraemer, Lois Kraemer, Renee Mattingly, Brent Mattingly, Donnie Martin, Lindsey Backes, Merrill Burnett, Linda Murphy, Cindy Opp, Natasha Waterstradt, Diane Waterstradt, Christian Waterstradt, Jacob Waterstradt, Charles Waterstradt, Angie Pierce, Ryan Pierce, Kalee Pierce, Clem Penrose, Stacey Taylor, Blade Taylor, Kaiden Taylor, Reba Downen, Courtney Downen, Brenda Cross, Brian Mooney, Cecilia's Golden Rose, John Omiotek, Clem Brown, Marla Heifner, Asjia Oneal, Christine LaGore, Charlene Vierhile, Laura Cler, Hannah Cler, Maddie Cler, Kyla Hook, Ashton Hook, Barbara Ulrich, Gerry Ulrich, Ella Hutchins, Van Den Broek Girls, Dr. Michael Dreith

Closed